Welcome!

Join the club!

Music

Math

Geography

Foreign Languages

Science

Phonics

Social Studies

Logic

Word Play

Tad's Scrapbook

Discover Tad's favorite animals!

Ladybug

Do all birds fly?

Penguin

Giraffe

Raccoon

How many bones in a shark?

Shark

GO

STOP

growl

Tiger

Parrot

What's an insect?

Bee

Owl

Who can see in the dark?

Elephant

games

Math Mania

Count your way through the spooky house!

GO

STOP

games

Wiggly Worms!

Create your own silly poem.

Web

Snail

Mushroom

Boot

Twig

Pretzel

Worm

Star

Yo-Yo

> Want to be a [   ]?
> Let's do the . . .
> Get down in the [   ].
> Wiggle in your. . .

Dirt

Squirm

Shirt

games

The Seven Continents
of the World

GO

Arctic Ocean

North America

Atlantic Ocean

Pacific Ocean

BUENOS AIRES – 6PM MONDAY

DALLAS – 4PM MONDAY

EQUATOR

South America

Pacific Ocean

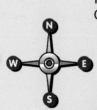

N
W E
S

Atlantic Ocean

Antarctica

STOP

fun facts

music

OSLO – 11PM MONDAY

Arctic Ocean

Europe

Asia

Pacific Ocean

Africa

BANGKOK – 4AM TUESDAY

Indian Ocean

Australia

NAIROBI – 12AM TUESDAY

MELBOURNE – 7AM TUESDAY

Antarctica

games

MONSTER SQUAD

K.C.   Tiger   Candy   Buzz   Stinkytoes

 "Well, what are we waiting for? Let's go catch a monster!"

 "The book says we have to follow the steps."

 "Yeah, we have to follow the steps!"

 "What's *she* doing here? This meeting is for Monster Squad members only!"

 "Sorry, guys. Mom says we have to include my little sister."

 read it

 "Oh, we're happy to let K.C. join the club. Aren't we, Tiger?"

 "Sure! If she doesn't mind being chased by terrible, snorting, growling, burping monsters who could gobble her up in one bite!"

 "You guys don't scare me. Besides, *I'm* the one who found the monster book in the first place."

 "OK, OK. Step number one: Find a swing set."

"Step number two: Jump up and down while shouting 'Stinkytoes! Stinkytoes! Stinkytoes!'"

"No way! That's baby stuff!"

"It says this particular monster called Stinkytoes likes to sing and play on swing sets. But the only way to see and hear him is to follow step number two."

"We are way too cool to do step number two."

"Stinkytoes! Stinkytoes! Stinkytoes!"

"Leave it to the baby to act like a baby."

STOP

read it

 "Hey! There he is!"

 "There who is?"

 "What would you guys do if you caught this monster anyway?"

 "Put him in jail, of course, silly."

 "But what if he's a nice monster?"

 "There's no such thing! That's why we're so important. We catch pesky monsters and make the world a better place."

 "Mmmm. Smells like Mom's baking chocolate chip cookies. Let's go!"

GO

STOP

read it

"You wouldn't gobble anyone up, would you, Stinkytoes?"

 "Well, I *am* very hungry."

 "W-w-what are you h-h-hungry f-f-for?"

 "A chocolate chip cookie."

 "That's all? You don't want to eat me?"

 "Blechhh! That's disgusting!"

 "You're funny, and you know what else?"

 "What else?"

 "I just figured out why they call you Stinkytoes!"

  game.

The Green Grass Grew All Around

Oh, in___ the woods there was a tree, the

pre - tti - est tree that you e - ver did see. And the

tree was in the ground, and the green grass grew all a -

round, all a-round, and the green grass grew all a - round.

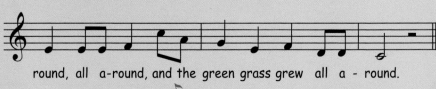

play   game.

Word Wizard

Create a fun sentence! Touch a blue word, a purple word, and a green word.

Wet

fly.

pups

GO

Fuzzy

nap.

hippos

Wobbly

jump.

frogs

 STOP

 games

say it spell it sound it

Word Bubbles!

Find the words hidden in the bubbles.

N	E	T	M	A	T
H	Y	R	C	D	F
N	A	P	T	A	P
H	O	T	S	U	B
A	L	B	T	U	B
E	W	E	T	O	P

NET MAT TUB

TAP HOT NAP

WET SUB TOP

TEN PAT PAN

BUS BUT POT

say it | sound it | ABC games

MONSTER FAMILY TREE

VAMPS

BUMPY

BONES

CREEPY

HAIRY

ICKY

?

ICKY 1

ICKY 2

ICKY 3

Who's your
favorite
monster?

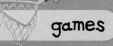

¡Hola Amigos!

Let's learn Spanish!

el pájaro

los zapatos

la niña

el monopatín

los pantalones

la mariposa

el perro

GO

STOP

games

The Four Seasons

Some trees stay green all year. Others change with the seasons. Look at how this tree changes.

Spring

Buds grow and turn into leaves.

Summer

The tree is full of green leaves.

Winter

The tree rests. It saves energy.

Fall

Leaves turn color and fall off.

GO

STOP

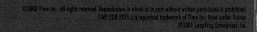

games

A Bear's Year Grizzly bears eat like crazy in the summer and fall. In the winter they rest, and their cubs are born. In the spring the cubs grow and play.

Summer

Fall

Winter

Spring

How Much?
~~~~ II

You'd have to eat 42 hamburgers in a day to eat as much as a bear in fall.

game

Wacky Farm

Find 15 strange things in this picture.

GO

STOP

HOMEMADE ICE CREAM

games

Welcome to the LeapPad® Library!

LeapFrog®
LEAP•START
Preschool-K • Up to Age 5

 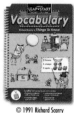  

© 1991 Richard Scarry

LEAP•START Books:
Reading Readiness and Simple Activities

LeapFrog®
LEAP•1
Preschool-Grade 1 • Ages 4-6

LEAP•1 Books:
Learning to Read and Introduction to Simple Subjects

© 1999 Disney Enterprises, Inc.   ™ & © 1998 Hanna-Barbera   © 1999 Scholastic, Inc.

LeapFrog®
LEAP•2
Grades 1-3 • Ages 6-8

LEAP•2 Books:
Reading Practice and School-Related Subjects

© 1998 Marc Brown   ™ & © 2001 DC Comics   © 2001 Disney/Pixar

LeapFrog®
LEAP•3
Grades 3-5 • Ages 8-10

  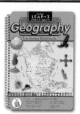 

LEAP•3 Books:
Reading Comprehension and Reading to Learn